STEGOSAURUS

BY SUSAN H. GRAY · ILLUSTRATED BY ROBERT SQUIER

The Child's World

Published in the United States of America by The Child's World®
1980 Lookout Drive • Mankato, MN 56003-1705
800-599-READ • www.childsworld.com

ACKNOWLEDGMENTS
The Child's World®: Mary Berendes, Publishing Director
The Design Lab: Kathleen Petelinsek, Art Direction and Design;
Victoria Stanley and Anna Petelinsek, Page Production
Editorial Directions: E. Russell Primm, Editor; Lucia Raatma, Copy Editor;
Dina Rubin, Proofreader; Tim Griffin, Indexer

PHOTO CREDITS
©Alysta/Dreamstime.com: cover, 2–3; ©Bettmann/Corbis: 4; ©Francois
Gohier/Photo Researchers, Inc.: 8 (top); ©A.J. Copley/Visuals Unlimited,
Inc.: 8–9; ©Miniben/Dreamstime.com: 12–13; ©Ken Lucas/Visuals
Unlimited, Inc.: 15; ©Science, Industry & Business Library/New York Public
Library/Science Photo Library/Photo Resesarchers, Inc.: 16 (top); ©Dave G.
Houser/Corbis: 16–17

LIBRARY OF CONGRESS CATALOGING-IN-PUBLICATION DATA
Gray, Susan Heinrichs.
  Stegosaurus / by Susan H. Gray; illustrated by Robert Squier.
    p. cm.
  Includes bibliographical references and index.
  ISBN 978-1-60253-242-7 (lib. bound: alk. paper)
  1. Stegosaurus—Juvenile literature. I. Squier, Robert, ill. II. Title.
  QE862.O65G74582 2009
  567.915'3—dc22   2009001631

TABLE OF CONTENTS

WHAT WAS STEGOSAURUS?

Stegosaurus (steg-uh-SAWR-uss) was a big, bulky dinosaur. It weighed more than a pickup truck! It had large, pointed plates on its back. They stood up in two rows. Those plates are a **mystery**. No one knows what they were for.

Stegosaurus *was gigantic. Just look how big its foot is compared to this museum visitor (above)!*

WHAT DID *STEGOSAURUS* LOOK LIKE?

Stegosaurus had a little head and a short, thick neck. Its legs were sturdy like an elephant's legs. The dinosaur's tail was its only **weapon**. It had big **spikes** on the end. Other dinosaurs thought twice before attacking *Stegosaurus*. They did not want to mess with that tail!

Stegosaurus *was mostly a peaceful dinosaur. It was strong enough to defend itself in a fight, though.*

WHAT ABOUT THOSE PLATES?

The plates were hard and bony. They had little holes and tunnels inside. **Scientists** think the tunnels held **blood vessels**. Perhaps the plates helped *Stegosaurus* with its **temperature**.

Scientists aren't sure why Stegosaurus had plates. One day, they hope to solve this mystery.

On chilly days, maybe *Stegosaurus* felt cold. To warm up, it stood out in the sunlight. Then the plates heated up. The blood inside warmed up, too. On hot days, maybe *Stegosaurus* stood in the shade. Then the plates and blood cooled down.

Maybe the plates just made *Stegosaurus* look bigger. That would scare other dinosaurs away.

Scientists have many different guesses about why Stegosaurus *had plates. Some believe they were used to control the dinosaur's body temperature.*

WHAT WAS *STEGOSAURUS'* DAY LIKE?

Stegosaurus spent most of its day eating. Big meals made the dinosaur sleepy. So it also took lots of naps.

Stegosaurus was not a hunter. It was not a fierce **predator**. Instead, it just ate plants.

A lush area with lots of plants would have been a good place for Stegosaurus to live. Then the dinosaur would always have had plenty to eat.

13

Stegosaurus' lips were hard like a bird's beak. They could rip a bush right out of the ground. They could tear the branches from trees. Perhaps Stegosaurus reared up on its hind legs to eat. Then it could reach leaves that were up high.

Stegosaurus' body and head were designed for eating plants. This dinosaur would not have been able to chew meat.

HOW DO WE KNOW ABOUT *STEGOSAURUS?*

Scientists have found **fossils** of *Stegosaurus*. They have found its bones and teeth. They have found its plates and tail spikes.

Othniel Charles Marsh (above) named the Stegosaurus. Scientists work hard to put Stegosaurus bones back together the right way (right).

In Colorado, scientists found a great *Stegosaurus* **skeleton**. One of the spikes looked unusual. Scientists think the dinosaur had been injured. The *Stegosaurus* was probably hurt in a fight. What a tough life the dinosaurs had!

Scientists keep looking for new Stegosaurus *fossils. They want to learn even more about this dinosaur.*

WHERE HAVE STEGOSAURUS BONES BEEN FOUND?

Colorado

Portugal

India

Asia

NORTH AMERICA

EUROPE

ASIA

Atlantic Ocean

Pacific Ocean

AFRICA

Africa

SOUTH AMERICA

Indian Ocean

AUSTRALIA

Map Key

Where *Stegosaurus* bones have been found

Where possible *Stegosaurus* fossils or tracks have been found

Southern Ocean

WHO FINDS THE BONES?

Fossil hunters find dinosaur bones. Some fossil hunters are scientists. Others are people who hunt fossils for fun. They go to areas where dinosaurs once lived. They find bones in rocky places, in mountainsides, and in deserts.

When fossil hunters discover dinosaur bones, they get busy. They use picks to chip rocks away from the fossils. They use small brushes to sweep off any dirt. They take pictures of the fossils. They also write notes about where the fossils were found. They want to remember everything!

Fossil hunters use many tools to dig up fossils. It is very important to use the right tools so the fossils do not get damaged.

GLOSSARY

blood vessels (*BLUD VESS-ullz*) Blood vessels are narrow tubes inside the body through which blood flows.

fossils (*FOSS-ullz*) Fossils are preserved parts of plants and animals that died long ago.

mystery (*MISS-tur-ee*) A mystery is something that no one can figure out.

predator (*PRED-ah-tur*) A predator is an animal that hunts and eats other animals.

scientists (*SY-un-tists*) Scientists are people who study how things work through observations and experiments.

skeleton (*SKEL-uh-tun*) The skeleton is the set of bones in a body.

spikes (*SPIKES*) Spikes are large, sharp, pointed things.

Stegosaurus (*steg-uh-SAWR-uss*) *Stegosaurus* was a large dinosaur with plates on its back.

temperature (*TEM-pur-ah-chur*) The temperature of something is a measurement of how hot or cold it is.

weapon (*WEP-un*) A weapon is an instrument used for attacking something else.

BOOKS

Bentley, Dawn. *A Busy Day for Stegosaurus*.
Norwalk, CT: Soundprints, 2004.

Bentley, Dawn. *Surprise, Stegosaurus!*
Norwalk, CT: Little Soundprints, 2004.

Landau, Elaine. *Stegosaurus*.
New York: Scholastic, 2007.

Mattern, Joanne. *Stegosaurus*. Norwalk, CT:
Weekly Reader Early Learning Library, 2007.

WEB SITES

Visit our Web site for lots of links about *Stegosaurus*:
CHILDSWORLD.COM/LINKS

Note to Parents, Teachers, and Librarians: We routinely verify our Web links to make sure they are safe, active sites—so encourage your readers to check them out!

INDEX

ABOUT THE AUTHOR

Susan Gray has written more than ninety books for children. She especially likes to write about animals. Susan lives in Cabot, Arkansas, with her husband, Michael, and many pets.

ABOUT THE ILLUSTRATOR

Robert Squier has been drawing dinosaurs ever since he could hold a crayon. Today, instead of using crayons, he uses pencils, paint, and the computer. Robert lives in New Hampshire with his wife, Jessica, and a house full of dinosaur toys. *Stegosaurus* is his favorite dinosaur.